OUT OF THE WEEDS

A Book of Poetry

By
Heather D. Pease

TEMPESTUOUS *(adj.) - Life filled with variety, of love, joy, beauty, hate, fear, and pain.*

© 2020 by **Heather D. Pease**

All rights reserved. No part of this publication may be reproduced, distributed or transmitted in any form or by any means, without prior written permission, except in the case of brief quotations embodied in articles and interviews.

Cover Design: Iram Shahzadi ("aaniyah.ahmed"99designs)

Out of the Weeds/ Pease, Heather -- 2nd edition
ISBN 978-0-578-65014-2

For Shay & Janae,
I love **all** that you are, have been, and will be.
I will be here for all of it!
I am so proud of you!

Pages to Pluck

BLOOMING..7
    How to Give a Flower...8
    Heather..10
    Morning Quenches My Thirst..11
    Big Apple Virgin..12
    One, Four, Three...14
    Transform..16
    Fine Art..17
    No, Not Today...18
    Expectations..20
    Talk to Me...22
    It Started as My Favorite Day..23

UNFOLDING..25
    A Room Too Small..26
    Rocks..28
    Insight – A List of Fears..30
    The Rotting Place..31
    Morning Rush..32
    Generations..33
    Everything is Fine..35
    #Believed...36
    Happy Thoughts..39
    Forget Me Not..40
    Nothing Left...41
    Good Night Conversation..42
    Monster Squatter...43

    I Took a Shower Today.. 45

    1,161 Days Between Orgasms... 47

    Walls.. 49

    Choices...49

    Arrow.. 49

FLOURISHES... **51**

    So, you know…... 52

    What I Want... 53

    Wonder Womxn.. 54

    Lips... 54

    Ache... 54

    Quickie.. 54

    A Season of Boyfriends.. 55

    No One Else... 57

    The Seven... 58

    Yearning.. 62

    Ruin My Lipstick.. 64

THE GARDEN... **65**

    Blank Page.. 66

    Uninspired Joy.. 67

    Meditation.. 68

    His Eyes.. 70

    The Twinkle in His Eyes.. 71

    Catfish & Hush Puppies... 73

    Jack's Legacy... 76

    Child Seat... 77

    Making the Bed.. 79

    Ask Again... 81

    Love Bug Longing... 82

    Poetic Girl.. 83

    Glorious.. 84

    Nectarine Summer... 86

My Gift.. 87

Permanent Ink... 89

Hummingbird's Union... 90

WILDFLOWERS...91

Who Plucks from My Pages?..92

Boundaries... 94

The When..95

Mine..96

Woman.. 98

Writer's Block..99

Words... 100

The Library... 101

Moments... 103

No Name... 105

Lessons from Life... 107

Writer... 110

PETALS OF GRATITUDE... 112

Chapter One

BLOOMING

MERAKA (v.) - *To have passion, or love. To put something of yourself into your work.*

How to Give a Flower

A dandelion,
to wish for
better days.

A plucked thistle,
to press in a book
a happy revisit.

Bright pink carnation,
to remind you
of my lips.

Gardenia memories,
for my nose to breathe,
a grounding.

A single daisy,
as a gentle nudge
to smile.

Dried lavender,
to tuck in my pillow
for restful sleep.

Bunches of daffodils,
bright and full
of potential.

Amaryllis' hardy bloom,
to welcome in
joyful days ahead.

Heather, to remind me
of good days, good people,
of how to see myself as lucky.

Hydrangeas, because you
understand small things
light the darkest days.

When I die, do not fill the house
with grave arrangements.
Sprinkle my ashes
among the wildest of flowers,
so I may grow again.

Heather

Born in the sweet kiss of summer—
a region the world has derided.
A little wild flower.
Dangerous. Essential. Demanding.

Our hope.

Morning Quenches My Thirst

Breeze carries crisp cut
grass; my nose becomes hearty
with Spring.
Sunbeams target dewdrops
with lasers creating
a captured firework
sparkler on each leaf.
Flowers bask as flowers do.
Squirrels frolic, tails twitch,
as they gossip frantically across limbs.
Butterflies float on a breath—
a dainty, delirious dance.
A robin sits on a lamppost,
boasting plump, proud plumage.
Bobs its head, flaps
wings, sways, satiated, smug,
after its early morning meal.
My coffee sits, untouched.

Big Apple Virgin

My day begins—a click-clack-click
of the train's sleepy approach,
sliding into Grand Central Station.
The sound of tap-tap-tap-tap, shoes clamoring,
a chaotic echo bouncing
between towering marble columns,
abrupt
in their urgency.

I am swept into a beautifully choreographed dance,
watching giant letters on arrival and departure boards
flip–flip–flip-flipping furiously every few seconds.
This is no lasting place, but a coming and going
of goodbyes and hellos; a sprawling constellation
of gold and blue heavens;
a façade
too soon realized.

Stepping into streets pouring
with people, arms above heads sans umbrellas—
some using newspapers, wet with different forecasts.

Raindrops thick enough to catch in a hand.
They puddle
before evaporating in the heat,
turning into a sweat,   instead of relief.
They bounce off hot pavements, as if scorched,
with an upward splash.

Thunder ricochets off buildings,
taller than clouds, bouncing
from one to another—

a 13th-story origin that quickly disappears
around a corner, late for a Broadway show.
The street smells wet, a cocktail
of tar, rock, gasoline, and rubber.
Break lights beam rows and rows and rows, highlighting
the rush.

The rain stops as quickly as it came, disappearing
into thin air, leaving a mugginess,
semi-comfortable in its uncomfortable uniformity.
Routine instantly returns to the city,
a regularity of horns blaring, slick roads.
Yet, everything seems brighter, gleaming
neon, sparkling subway grates releasing
a cooler steam—relief from below.

A beggar sits against a streetlight.
His sign reads, "Need money, for food, a drink,
and Pot (hey, at least I'm honest)."
He smiles and points, saying,
Times Square is that way. Welcome to New York.

One, Four, Three

Don't say it. Hold it tight, close
to your own heart.
Don't let it break away from lips, only
to be scattered to the
universe, forever
out there, raw,
unprotected by silence.

Don't let it leave your embrace,
fall upon ears that do
not hear.
Don't let it bleed and stab you
with pain
once spoken.
However, if you say it…

Don't hold it back or hold it in
until you explode.
Unable to contain the commitment
of its meaning;
once pronounced
as it　　　lingers
at the boundary of
your tongue.

Don't rehearse it before
you declare it to tender ears.
Don't let another second pass
without them
knowing,
every day,
for eternity.

Don't forget how you feel
in this moment.
Don't doubt it, once delivered.
Don't ever stop believing in it,
no matter how cliché.

Don't pass it around
or it will lose its magic.
Or forget it ignites
everything wondrous.
Don't take it back,
once articulated upon their heart.
And never let it go
without a kiss.

Transform

Transform them
into a sonnet.
Make each freckle on their skin
a poem.
Compose and adore them,
with prose.
And they will run
into your arms,
without hesitation.
Then you both will be
poetry.

Fine Art

I would like to stand naked
while admiring fine art.
My left arm draped
lazily over my head.
Hair pulled up,
exposing my neck.
My right index finger
between my teeth.
I am in deep
thought.
Gaining a new perspective.
Exploring new possibilities
of inspiration.

But the idea
of being arrested
tends to hinder my experience.
Restrict my enjoyment.
Limit my devotion
to any great masterpiece.
So, I admire fine art,
like everyone else,
with just a naked eye.

No, Not Today

My muse sensed
new love
in my heart.
In a fragment
of a lonely minute,
giving up my secret,
with a single breathless sigh.

Feelings never behave
when I ask 'em to.
Always controlling
my darn thoughts.
Lettin' me drift,
into the safety
of his smile.

His innocent
day-dreamy kisses
captivate me.
Then the sensible me forgets
to tell my ecstatic heart
he is not reachable.

No, not today.
Love is so exquisite
when it's new.
He perfectly

fills my emptiness.
I can't break my heart;
just now.

Maybe,
I'll tell me
tomorrow.

Expectations

Of you?
I have none.
None,
that will hold you
to a lifetime.

Nothing to tie you down
and leave my hands
clinging to your being,
gripped tightly, smothering
your freedom.

Your life, sifting through
the claws of ownership
so easily outstretched,
where trembling hearts
are caught like flies in a web.

I have no intentions
of laying my snare in your path.
Holding you down,
bargaining your life
for intrigue and enchantment.

Perhaps, somehow, just maybe,
there could be a flicker?
A flame hidden within.

A mere desire to have you
be with me, willingly,
instead of like prey.

Expectations?
I have none.
Do not look into my eyes.
Turn around,
walk right out that door.

It's over there
just
through
my
heart.

Talk to Me

I hunger for strange jive.
For an unusual conference of gab.
A worthy partner prepared
for an exquisite exchange.
The coupling of minds delving deep
into a tongue only we can speak.
I want to parley until candles tire.

Talk to me. Make me guffaw.
Be irresponsible,
becoming drunk on words.
Undress my mind
with infinite conversation
of things that matter
or don't.

I desire to genuinely hear you,
for you to easily listen to me.
Catch each syllable, allow it
to tickle the finest parts of your ear.
Crave me
for my mind.

Sit beside me, let's
hold hands,
turn off the world around us,
and yarn words
into a blanket
we call our favorite.

It Started as My Favorite Day

Oh, Stop Sign, where did you hide?
How could I not heed
your bold, red, octagon,
warning me
to still myself
for a brief moment.

You protect me from dangers.
My oath to obey!
Guilty of ignoring your existence.
Oh, Stop Sign, release me;
this lapse in judgment.
Music blaring perfection;
I was singing along,

hands at six and, I don't remember.
Cruising along;
destination—an interesting brownstone.
Sun roof wide open, accepting Spring air.
Not a worry in the world.

Flashing lights behind,
mistaken blue skies
only on my radar.
Blissfully belting out lyrics,
a siren breaks
between stanzas.
The day, momentarily abrupt

in its seriousness.
Failure to stop.

A ticket to appear;
a fine.
Not fine.

Chapter Two

UNFOLDING

TACENDA *(n.) - Things better left unsaid; matters passed over in silence.*

A Room Too Small

I don't remember the sun on my skin.
There were no last wishes.
Nothing was supposed to be final yet.

The urn selected/its home,
a mantel.
Someone said it would be heavy   after.

The door creaked. Its knob ached/ as it turned
to a room not vast enough/ for all my sorrow.
Time froze/escape closed behind me/ pulling all
oxygen out with it.

The room - no bigger than a closet.
There were no flowers to comfort/no chair
to sit with my grief/ I didn't notice tissues/sitting
on a table.

There was a window/the curtain on the other side.
Nothing   under my control,
the room was considerate/ in its consciousness.

Someone out of reach drew drapes revealed my dad
on a table/ scratchy/ starched sheet at his chest, offered
no comfort.

He looked cold; I had no blanket to give. He should
be sleeping in his favorite chair/ this room, this
senseless --small room   full of silence, not

his snores. / I could hear my hands tremble.

I stared, anchored to regret /willing him
to be miraculous/not
become ash.

Rocks

I was only a pebble when my mom called me her rock
as we buried ours.
Rocks crumble when the   earth   quakes
Rubble left in the wake.
The strength of my family
turned gravel   then sand
sifted through hands   reached out
once anchored in love.

Being a rock felt like being thrown   through windows
everywhere I stepped--glass shards
in a quarry of sorrow.

My father collected rocks, sorted, and arranged them
to lean on each other
building a future, a community.

You see, rocks must live together;
that's why you see them in piles.
Lying in river beds, shaping the world
around them.
Creating mountains together.

Some rocks are worn on fingers
around necks to   glitter and   dazzle
cherished for their beauty.
Others must be cracked open   to reveal a
glorious core inside.

Certain rocks are created with   intense force
pressure-folded   and crushed

into a metamorphic form   of what they were before,
part of the original but
different.

I didn't know what kind of rock to be for her.
Was I meant to build   something new for us
or roll away?
Did she need me soft and smooth laying quietly;
or hard and jagged like flint?
Inside I was shattered into a million pieces.

I wasn't ready to be a rock,
I felt like a grain of sand
I was just   a person being strong
because someone told me I was
and I wanted to believe it too.

Insight – A List of Fears

Saying too much

or not enough.

Losing might.

Silence when discussion is needed.

Weakness in those I depend on for strength.

Losing him and them.

Tornadoes, shaking in closets.

My mom, reading my poetry.

The earth - quaking.

Rage that sits at the base of the spine.

Lies.

Religion -- man's interpretation, not faith.

Intolerance.

My mom *not* reading my poetry.

Losing self.

Global warming.

What we can't fix.

Triggers –- guns, not feelings.

Bees dying.

Suicide.

The Rotting Place

Cover the rotting place.
Make light
of the corpse
flower bloom.
It's pillowed petals
and crumbled dry
crusted tissues.
Sleep is a catnap,
with sharpened claws.
I crave the scratch.

Morning Rush

after Why Maggots by David Hernandez

Because I was washing dishes and wouldn't look.
Because my daughter always complained about eating. Because
I was tired and cranky and annoyed. Because my daughter
would be tardy to school again. Because I yelled shut up and eat
your cereal!

So my daughter cried and stopped complaining about bugs.
Tried to eat around them as they wiggled. Put her bowl on the
counter by the sink to put her shoes on so we wouldn't be late. I
picked up

the dish where they writhed among fruit and bran. Where they
swam in milk, only a tiny bit was left. Where I saw the maggots
in my daughter's food. Where tears of frustration had to wait.
Where sorry felt as uncomfortable as my daughter's stomach.

Generations

My daughter's mother
is not an alcoholic.
Neither is her mother.
That is how you break a pattern.
How you create hope
for a future. How you stop
a cycle from repeating
generations of drinking
and being beaten.

Of men pouring income
into a bottle, they empty
on payday. Of hitting,
of broken dishes. Of promises to stop
and still more bruises to hide.
Of rage, abuse, words spoken
and never taken back.
Of little children who turned
into adults, full of trauma
who never grew up.

I don't know what it is like
to have a father who is cruel.
Or to be banished from a family
for having a child. I don't know the little
girl she was before, whose father
drank and cursed and threw things.

I don't know what it was like
for that father, to have a mother die
by choice. To spare herself
one more day of beatings.

I don't know the girl
she was before.

Before five children and a drunk
husband. When she was sold
by her parents to pay
a debt. At age eight, alone,
on a boat, only a doll under her arm.

I know caution
of too much—too much fun,
too much drink.
Of losing choice
to a man
who didn't give one.
I know discretion, panicked eyes
full of ancestry and ghosts that haunt
a mother, a daughter, a grandmother,
a child, all in one.

I know rage, the beast
that shook the house
and silenced it. The daughter I was,
am, because monsters
still scare me.

I know how to ask
for help. How to teach
my daughters the same. I know the primal
need to protect.

The darkness that lingers
just beneath the skin.
Blood coursing through veins
of women surviving, still,
five generations later.

Everything is Fine

Let's start
with the truth.
I lie.
You, fooled
easily
by deception.
Read my face—
a blush can tell you
a thousand truths
if you know how
to read
a hue.
But you will believe
deceptive tongues.
Because my lies
are your truth.
What you want
to believe.
It's the words,
how they twist down
the canal of your ear.
Manipulation is
just changing the hand.
My poker face
hides dusty stores.
A life lived in parallel
of the one built
with bloodied hands.
Molding it into the
perfect picture
of happiness.

#Believed

The details that bring me here today are the ones I will never forget. They have been seared into my memory and haunted me.
　　　　　–Christine Blasey Ford, September 2018

    i.
I had no understanding of my body as a 10-year-old.
I am swimming, slippery, like a seal
and "uncle" is a net, grabbing my waist.
I wiggle away, he grabs my breast, I am caught.
Pressed against his rigid swimsuit, he thrust against me
Someone is taking a picture of us in the pool;
I am forced to smile.

No, a banned word, it isn't polite, it isn't nice.
I say no, I say stop, I say don't.
I am ignored.

    ii.
I am 15, it's hot, I don't want to walk home,
my boyfriend's friend offers.
I say ok.
He jokes he's going to rape me.
We are in the band room, people hear.
This is how he is, so we ignore the spaz.
He asks to come in, he asks for a beer,
takes it without my reply.
I'm on the couch, suddenly so is he.
The DA says it's my word against his—
his word was *consensual*,
mine was *rape*, as in not believed.

iii.
A bunch of friends are spending the weekend in Mexico.
Drinking, taking shots, playing pool.
One man is a friend of a friend, is odd.
I ignore him.
There is dancing, so much dancing.
He doesn't dance, he watches, he stares.
Tired, we crash in a hotel room, bodies everywhere.
I am not drunk, on the floor, sleeping in my clothes.
He is there, over me.
Jolt wake to fingers forceful in me, thick, rough
ripping my body from my bones.
The entire room sleeps.
I say no, I say stop, I say don't, I move.
I don't sleep.

iv.
My body never felt like a temple --
more convenience store, where men
squeezed me for my ripeness.
The bigger my body, the more space
for men to feel, tap, brush up against,
or probe in search of their own desire.
Jerry was a thief,
pilfering control, hijacking a spirit.
His pet names and bad-boy persona
used to dominate me.
Father of my unborn daughter,
he tries vainly to force a miscarriage
and brutally evade responsibility.

His mental abuse has left us both
with years of struggling to heal.

v.
I am beyond pissed; I am fucking livid.
I am sad and tired.

This is my truth.
I remember every moment
of every assault, never forgetting.
Trying to move on.
Having moved on.
Survived.
I deserve to be believed.

Happy Thoughts

This page left intentionally blank.

Forget Me Not

Grief is the price we pay for love. – Queen Elizabeth II

When the swift rot of my flesh is over
and only the slow rot of bones is left,
will you fancy a day when there is no rain?
Reflect on a memory filled with our laughter
or imagine me among demons?
Label me a lipless monster with gnashing teeth,
waiting to carve out my own eyes?
Will I be the pit in your stomach once peach
blossom, fruit ripe, and juicy, running down your cheeks?
Or odd voice? A stranger in your ear, whispering grief
can only happen where there is love. Truth turns
rose petals into thorns.
You would never plant a garden
where weeds could grow.

Nothing Left

We've not shared words,
nor air,
in a lifetime.
Or held each other
in a meaningful embrace.
When the end arrives
with its cacophony
of tears and sorrow,
where, sister, will you be?
Will you be no mouth,
no tongue, no throat?
Perhaps damp violets
of a deceitful Lark;
a facade of song?
Be gnashing in mind
while sharing blessings?
Mourn the life of a stranger,
pray me into *family* around company?
What will you do when
words no longer need you
to find them?

Good Night Conversation

Be quiet mind. Hush now. Stop talking.
Haven't you said enough? Mulling over
non-existent
conversations.
This chatter is
thundering.
Please mind,
quiet yourself.
Take a break from madness. I know
you are stressed. I honor this chaotic

insaneness, the endurance it takes to be
in this never-ending battle. Every single
night, trying
to be calm.
Let go. Find
peace. Just a
storm-less night
of needed silence.
I am praying for muted slumber. Begging
for a truce. Just one night to rest my soul.

Monster Squatter

Eviction of monsters
is an undertaking,
to banish a lurker, who pilfers
my body, makes it a domicile
occupied with all its triggers and trappings.
Scrawl-filled walls line my chest heavy
with its skewed slant.

It whispers dark exaggerations, filling
me with toxic epilogue. I hear its heavy
steps in restless slumber.
Wake up abruptly to the click
of its jaw, see piles of clothes scattered
by its enormous tail, knowing it has found
real estate under the bed.
Claws hovering just there, near ankles
left exposed.

My wary eyes stare
at jagged shadows on the wall
resembling prison bars.
This wraith slyly shifts
into my head; acquiring
unendurable space.
I no longer want to lease myself
to this squatter; all its dense,
clump shrubs and twining
creepers making me doubt
my existence.

A slippery seducer

it behaves on occasion,
begging to dress up for dinner
but I no longer crave its company.
Foreclosure, mandatory.
Doors to close, access to deny,
locks to change,
self to protect, to take
repossession of my soul.
To live
without fear.

I Took a Shower Today

Turned the water on scald.
Stood underneath
until my skin turned pink,
just to feel something.

I took a shower today.
Picked my favorite
island scented gel and
squeezed it over a puff.
Rubbed my arms, breasts,
waist, legs, and back.
Covered my skin with bubbles.
I always avoid my belly.

I took a shower today.
Washed my hair
and my face.
Shaved my legs
and that ridiculous hair
on my big toe.

I took a shower today.
Stood body facing the shower head,
holding myself.
Letting water drench,
drip like hot tears
I am too numb to cry.

I took a shower today.
Stayed until fingertips pruned,
then even longer.

Lingered until steam
filled the room,
creating clouds
I want to sleep on.
Instead, I am in the middle
of a storm.

I took a shower today.
Turned off the water.
Dried myself
with a fluffy soft towel.
Put on my favorite perfume.
Felt my skin cool
and took
a deep breath.

1,161 Days Between Orgasms

Female Sexual Dysfunction (n.): *Inability to orgasm under any circumstances; the absence of sexual climax; lack of orgasm.*

> He unbuttons my jeans,
> zipper slowly comes down.
> Grabs my waist;
> loops fingers through where there is no belt.
> Slides them down over full hips.

Cause (n.): *The source of, or reason for, an action; that which produces or effects a result.*

> Sweat slides off bodies;
> blind lips find each other.
> Sheets stick; hands scrape
> along my back, causing pain
> I do not feel.

Dysfunction (n.): *A failure to function in an expected or complete manner.*
Dysfunction (v.): *To fail to function correctly; to malfunction.*

> My legs wrap around his waist, trying
> in vain to get a firm hold.
> Our bodies rock to a beat
> only we can hear.
> My hips grind against his.
> Each bump moves closer to…

Inability (n.): *Lack of the ability to do something; incapability. Psychological factors such as guilt, anxiety, or a past sexual trauma or abuse. Some medication side effect.*

...the edge disappears as if it was
never there.
I lie flat, hot tears streaming
down flushed cheeks.
Confused at my body,
its denial of satisfaction.

Incapable (adj.): *Not capable (of doing something); unable; not in a state to receive; not receptive; not susceptible; not able to admit.*

I feel   less   than   human
Knowing the need,
the want.
Plundered of feeling, ego
assaulted.

Absence (n.): *A state of being away or withdrawn; failure to be present where one is expected, wanted, or needed; a deficiency.*

Stolen sensuality.
Seductress mourned as passion died
Exclusion of release, leaving me
in constant...

Want (n.): *A desire, wish, longing (of) lack, absence; something needed or desired; a thing of which the loss is felt.*

No moan escaping from parted lips.
No sinking into ecstasy.
No invitation to oblivion.
No plunging into the abyss.
No tsunami of passion.
Sex loiters in the air,
feeling like I'll nev—

Walls

How thick do you build
barriers of racism?
Hatred on display!

Choices

Thwap, snap, tap the keys.
Letters turn words before you.
Love or hate, a choice

Arrow

No longer target
Bow ready, no quiver – aim
I. Am. The. Arrow.

Chapter Three

FLOURISHES

APODYOPSIS (v.) - *The act of mentally undressing someone.*

So, you know…

I am completely, absolutely,
from beginning to end,
fully, heart and soul,
hook line and sinker,
in all, all in, entirely,
in full, in toto,
on all counts,
to the nth degree,
totally, unanimously,
unconditionally, undividedly,
utterly, wholly,
and without omission

enjoying your smile
right now.

What I Want

Do not kiss me
with light feather kisses.
Instead, pull me close
with strength.
Press your lips
upon mine
with fierce, passionate
pressure.
Make me know
how you require
my mouth.
Brand me
with your
desire, burning
from your very essence.
Illustrate your craving
with lips
and tongue.
Pull me closer.
Wrap me in a strong embrace.
Take my hair and pull it hard.
Devour me
with a kiss or don't
even bother.

Wonder Womxn

Make me climax like
the Wonder Womxn I am.
Cum, the Amazon.

Lips

Come hither, my muse.
Your lips, fucking poetry.
On mine, a sonnet.

Ache

Fingertips brush skin.
Artist strokes slowly, down spine.
Goosebumps reveal ache.

Quickie

What time does it start?
Right now, I need you in me,
and we, are ne'er late.

A Season of Boyfriends

Spring

He was gorgeous and quick.
A breath of fresh air.
The beginning of warmth on my skin.
We danced in warm rain.
I wanted more of him,
for him to stay.
But before I could say more,
he was gone.

Summer

He was easy, breezy.
Sipping sangria on the beach.
Skin so perfectly kissed,
it was hard not to have sex with him
every moment of the day.
He looked so beautiful without clothes,
but was just light and fluffy clouds.
Once the season changed, he did too
The moment it got cold
so did his feelings.

Fall

Oh, he was so nice, too nice.
Immediately charmed by his sweetness,
I wanted to drink him
like warm chocolate with a spoon.
I imagined slow jazz when he was in the room.

The nights were so nice, long
and always leaving me wanting more.
Conversations so colorful, he could reach
into the depths of my mind.
We took wonderful strolls in the park,
but there were ball games, lots of ball games!
And the days became short.
Yes, he was stable but
he had to go. His niceness killed
desire. It was starting to snow.

Winter

All hail this amazing boyfriend;
once found, such a keeper.
No one likes being single when it is cold out.
With him, I could feast on whatever I pleased.
We stayed in and got drunk on mulled wine.
I was warmed from the top of my tongue to the
fireplace below my belly button.
His winter coat was there to wrap around me.
I felt comforted in his embrace.
He rescued me from the dark.
Loved me in thirty-degree weather.
He was a gift!

No One Else

Women are taught
to always want
a chivalrous prince.
But right now,
something
about you
has me
feeling
like lightning.
Striking me
at the edge of night,
where desire lingers.
Making my head weak.
The lust in me
burns brightly.
I feel like I am on fire!
And it was you
that stirred
the embers
of carnal desires.
Both of us need
to release this
tension.
I am burning pleasure.
No one else
will do.

The Seven

Lust

Thoughts of you linger / and tempt / and flirt / with my psyche/ Make me ache for fingers / and lips / and grabs / and thrusts / that grind until dawn / or exhaustion / whichever comes first.

Gluttony

Ravenous for your fingers, plunging
deep, inside me.
Slipping
and sliding.
Building a desire,
a deluge all over
your hand,
penetrating me to my core.
I am frenzied for your cock
to fill me, feed me.
The back of my throat
requires your fullness.
I hunger for more—
satiation impossible.
Touch me.
Fuck me.
Make me cum again
and again and
again!

Greed

Address me, Avarice.
Let luxury fondle your tongue.
Fuck religion, worship me!
I will grant your every desire.
Let you lounge in my rich embrace.
Giving you a wealth of satisfaction.
Lie at my feet, put your trust in me.
Lose your mind in my excess.
Be my fool.
I'm so worth it.

Sloth

My mind anguishes
in your sluggish tease,
cherishing the slow,
lazy but deliberate way
your hand idles.
Takes lethargic
time, sliding over
bare breast,
creating bumps
on my skin.
Sending shivers
coursing
down
my
spine.
I'm a junkie
for the awakening.
Quaking underneath
your touch.
My body
turns feverish.

Your disinclination
to action, to feel
my skin
quiver,
makes the want
insatiable.

Wrath

I want to rip off your jeans / slam your body on the bed / Mount you / Lean down / bite your ear / until you yelp in pain /Tie your hands / above your head / and ride you / hard / Make your cock / fucking mine / Don't you dare / close your eyes / shut / your mouth / Don't speak / you pretty thing / I am still / pissed.

Envy

Tell me how you fuck her.
Is it different than me?
Does her heart beat faster for you?
Is her pussy sweeter?
Can she taste me on your cock?
You were so deep inside.
I covet her lips to taste you again.
To explode, feel the electricity of us
run through my veins.
Your hips grinding against mine.
For my lips to be your only kiss.
Why can't you
be
with just
me?

Pride

I love my tits, my ass, my cunt, your cock, your thighs, your shoulders, your eyes. How they fit together, like puzzle pieces, of fingers, and toes, and mouths, and legs that spoon. How I cum for you and you cum for me, and we cum together. In the morning or afternoon. An evening. Sometimes until dawn, when naughty and nasty are the same as love, trust and us.

Yearning

Strip me. From your knees.
Yank unbuttoned jeans over ample hips.

Hook fingers onto my panties, and slide them
slowly down to my ankles. Fling them to the side.

Lock cornflower blue eyes with green; a silent conversation.
Your mouth so close, my hips shift at your smolder.

Push me onto the bed. Remove my shirt, overhead. Tie my
wrists to the headboard, the one we picked out, just for this.

Bite my neck. Build shivers on flesh, urging you to take your
time. Undulate your tongue over nipples erect, with necessity.

Make me grit my teeth and squeal, watching you move
lower. No one has mastered me like this.

Caress my belly button from between thighs;
with your mouth, there, oh, so, fucking there.

Require me to submit my body to a skilled devil.
This fallen angel who loves my clit for the woman she is.

Make me twisted with apocalyptic pleasure, creating an inferno
inside bones. Don't stop, don't   fucking   stop.

Seize me with hands. Grip and fondle. Mold me into a cup,
quenching an insatiable thirst.

Pace me with taste and procrastination.

Control a tide until you make me drown oceans.

Kiss me, messing blood red lips with slick, delicious wetness.
Whisper vows of appetite, of desire, of cravings—small deaths.

Do exactly what I like, times two.

Ruin My Lipstick

Ruin my lipstick—
not my mascara tear eyes—
with firm craze kisses.

Paint your passion, please,
on each fold of my body,
accepting my gift.

Make love to my soul
without touching my ego.
Leave it whole, unbruised.

Show me you see me
truly inside, behind eyes
where I hide from you.

Do not accept *I am fine.*
Tear down walls with love.

Chapter Four

THE GARDEN

REDAMANCY *(n.) - The act of loving the ones who love you; a love returned in full.*

Blank Page

The man who
loves me
writes his
love
on my soul,
like I write
poetry
on
paper.

Uninspired Joy

I really enjoy
the quiet times.
Uninspired
by the twists and turns of life.
The calm.
Mind at ease.
Joy? Perhaps.
I smile
at the thought
of enjoyment,
quietness,
peacefulness,
and ease.
A vacation
without rollercoasters.
Finding calm,
stretching time, becoming
soul quenched.

Meditation

Serene pond sprawling;
a grounding of water.
Ducks meandering joy,
rippling in an endless mirror.
I am mesmerized.

Trees dot-to-dot before me.
Each twisty and bendy,
begging for a climb.
To live
in this moment.

Gossamer breeze
fills my nose
with the sweetness
of fresh cut grass,
reminding me to breathe.

Breathe and release
anticipation.
Enjoy the bloom.
See the petals of each flower,
leaves on each bush,
the lizard scampering across the path.

Hear fuzzy bees buzzing—
feet swollen with pollen—
fluttering from flower to flower.
A syncopated dance;
I am envious of the whim.

Smell sweet plump purple
thistle, with velvet
leaves I take.
To capture
the moment.
To savor
this memory.

Press it into a book;
a totem to transport.
Turn a second
into a life-
time.

To reflect on
when peace is needed.
To quiet
a restless mind.
A meditation filling me
with calm.

His Eyes

Kind, gentle, like him.
Vivid, lakes of azure
and allure.
I brim at his wink.
Blush from his smolder.
A reflection of real love.
My darling is a sea
of contemplation, I want to swim
in for an eternity.

The Twinkle in His Eyes

At age five, with skinned knees
and messy hair, I climbed
on his lap; eyes full of wonder.
Begged for stuffed animals; a set mouth
promised -- I'd been good.

He knew the truth.
His eyes, familiar--yet not, twinkled
as he smiled from the tip of his spectacles

I looked back over my
shoulder, saying goodbye.
His gloved hand waved back.
The line of children stretched
around the store, yet I left feeling he knew me.
His lap felt like home, the crook
of his arm a hug.

At eight I asked for a cradle.
Santa promised late
nights in his workshop
Sanding, sculpting,
and creating a special
cradle just for me.

At age nine I peeked in
a forbidden window, peered through
dust. Saw sleigh bells on reindeer.
They pranced frozen in time,
each pulling red and gold sleigh.
Leather reins laid on ebony seat.

Awestruck, I memorized every detail.
Searched deep back closets --I found
it -- a large black bag unzipped
revealing a red suit.

And you might think the magic
would go. This revelation would cause
me to lose belief but no—
The magic of the season became
extraordinarily genuine.

Now clandestine, the illusion
mine to keep. In awe
of this man I thought I knew.
His twinkling eyes
confirmed Santa
lived with me.

Catfish & Hush Puppies

For my eighth birthday, my daddy
got me a fishin' pole.
White, with pink accents, and a huge
black button that made
castin' really fun.
Daddy put his arms around
me, big, like a bear, showin'
me how to reach back
don't let go and swing.
Pushin' button to hear
the zippin' then plop,
the bright white and orange bobble
floatin' while we waited
for a nibble.

I wanted to practice castin', leavin'
worms – man's work,
but no, his daughter would
know, how the biggest worms
make for better pluckin'
how piercin' it just right with a hook
then loopin' it around repeatin'
bein' careful not to hook
your thumb!

I sliced two worms in
half, he said, pick it back up
and wrap'em, don't waste'em.

I got good at this quickly
optin' for the fattest ones,

deep in the bottom of the Styrofoam
dirt-filled cup
with the word BAIT
handwritten in red caps.

Why do the fish I have to catch
like worms?
The fish daddy gets to catch
like peanut butter.

We sat there, all afternoon, a birthday
wish came true with sinkin'
bobble, reelin' in my catch, a perch,
then carp, a trout or two!
I was wantin' to catch
a catfish, them suckers liked
daddy's peanut butter.
I gotta few with Skippy!

He had me carry em' all, puttin'
em' in the blue cooler in the back
of our yellow pick-up.
Sittin' in the truck, listenin'
to somethin' country,
dreadin' the cleanin',
learnin' about the floater – inside!
Scrappin' scales, shimmerin' rainbows
flickin' off fallin' on the ground.
Daddy cut off
the heads and tails.

Inside the house, he becomes
chef, hot Crisco oil, hush puppies fryin',
fish bubble, crack, and pop
scaldin' perfection.
We ate all the fixins, leavin'

any bones on the plate.
My belly full - I went to bed dreamin'
of swimmin' like a fish,
lookin' for the biggest
worm in the lake.

Jack's Legacy

A giant weight I wish was his hug.
His leather jacket hangs in my closet.
My dad was a veteran and a cabinetmaker.
Could sing; played a beautiful six-string.
Was a sailor who fell in love with a girl in town.
He delivered me—
a true Father's Day gift.
A proud man, gentle and kind.
As his oldest, I am a lot like him,
although more outspoken.
We clashed often.
Me, difficult child, the black sheep.
My mouth, always the problem.
Both of us yelling
to be heard, never to listen.
Our relationship, strained.
His passing
almost killed me.
Dark years after, always, needing him.
I still do.
I miss our shared laughter.
Our similarities are mine to cherish now.
The gifts of stubbornness, strength,
and integrity, always!
Proud to be his legacy.
I wear his genes
like his leather jacket.

Child Seat

My mom is a cleaned house—
rearranged in the middle of the night.
My childhood happiness is
wrapped in her hug.
The curled crook of her knees
on the couch, my favorite spot.
I need her acceptance
like breath, like heartbeat.

My childhood happiness is
wrapped in her hug.
My giggles spurred as she pedaled down
country roads, me in the child seat.
I need her acceptance
like breath, like heartbeat.
She is the voice in my head that
comes out of my mouth.

My giggles spurred as she pedaled down
country roads, me in the child seat.
I love her, one more
beluga whale to her million.
She is the voice in my head that
comes out of my mouth.
She will always be the first
person I want to call when
something amazing happens!

I love her, one more
beluga whale to her million.
I still twirl/dance in the living room
to Simon & Garfunkel.

She will always be the first
person I want to call when
something amazing happens!
She is my fluffer nutter;
my let's get a pedicure
because football is on.

I still twirl/dance in the living room
to Simon & Garfunkel.
The curled crook of her knees
on the couch, my favorite spot.
She is my fluffer nutter;
my let's get a pedicure
because football is on.
My mom is a clean house
—rearranged in the middle of the night.
My childhood happiness is
wrapped in her hug.

Making the Bed

Aching eyes wake,
determined
not to shade myself
from beaming sunshine.
Stretching

my back, legs,
and arms high
above my head.
A smile on a mind
yet to reach lips.

Removing my cocoon
of supple, soft sheets. Wrapped
in a pretzel made
for deep slumber,
stirring

from sleep.
Standing. Straightening
dark sheets, I always hide here.
Putting lavender on my pillow,
for later.

Opening shutters, letting light
spread. Pulling
the comforter up all the way.
Allowing bright Bali colors
to please weary eyes.

Suddenly, dancing to music!

Hips moving side to side.
Dusting off small pillows. Only purpose?
To please me.
Un-souring my mouth.

Putting on a dress, twirling. Finding
myself laughing,
while putting away
gloomy notions.
Closing drawers and doors; leaving
the bed and starting the day.

Ask Again

Water engulfs toes
that sink
wet into quick sand.
Disappearing
in the tide.

Foam begs me…
to take a deeper step.
I deny its wish.
Stepping back,
only to tempt the wave
to ask
again.

Love Bug Longing

My cheek craves her kisses.
I beg, covering her with tight-lipped
gentle canoodles. Tickling her neck,
she leans in and giggles.
"Mmmmmmmooouuahhhhh," I say
her smile disappears
behind dimples I envy.
Her wide-open mouth
comes towards me,
lands its intended mark. Leaving me,
drenched in her love.
Her kiss lingers, glistens my cheek.
She falls into my arms;
leaving hope for time to stand still.
In a moment, she grows older.
Now, she kisses my forehead.
Uses two fingers, makes small circles
to rub it in, she says, flitting
off with friends.
Leaving a longing on my cheeks.
To glisten once more
with her love.
Her laugh tickles my ears.
I love the person she is becoming
before me.

Poetic Girl

I'm a plain girl.
Skin of pearl white.
My tongue hurls fierce spit.
Blunt words slit throats.

My shit worth more.
I'm a roar girl. A soar
so high - will not shy dreams.

Don't try to stop
me; my sharp bite.

A barbed wire girl.
Not your furl off
hide girl; but fight

for what's right girl.
A write my heart,
born for art, girl.
A part of me

to heal; free pain.
To see my life

full of rife girl.
I'm fife with flair
girl. I bare all
to share my soul

girl. I am whole.

Glorious

My body is glorious
in the dark.

Skin stretched to mask the pain
of unwanted glances,
touches, judgment.
It protects me.

My body says:
> *I know it is hard, but I*
> *am still here,*
> *fighting for us!*
> *Take care*
> *inside & out.*

Hooded eyes guarding
against a stranger's gaze.
Oh, how I long for a brief
smile or acknowledgement
of the bones beneath.

> *Darling, you are not*
> *your warped perception.*
> *I am trying*
> *to take care of you,*

Stretch marks like a map
of roads taken,
I hide them to forget
how they got there.

*Skin is just skin—
you are not your experiences.*

*We are only halfway
on this beautiful journey.
Thrilling adventures.
Tackling mountaintops.
Leaving behind childhood
roller coasters.*

*You are glorious
in the light.*

Nectarine Summer

Delightful juice
drips down my chin.
Sunshine captured
a small round treat,
hue of golden orange.
Ripened to perfection.
A juicy bite,
ready to be devoured—
every delightful bit.
Slurping pulp,
not to lose a drop of nectar bliss.
Summer comes alive.
Its extract savored
then gone.

My Gift

I remember falling in wonder
with the lobe of an ear, the curve
of a cheek, downy lashes resting on same.
A sleepy gaze staring up from the crook
of my heart. When my body became
nourishment, love's origin
was created out of their smile.

I remember unwrapping blankets bundling
bliss, extraordinary being,
tender in my arms. I will never let go!
This bond we share, was forged
the moment of our genesis.

I remember soft baby hair, laughter, teaching
butterfly kisses, melting for giggles. I still ache
when they shed tears. Their heart, strong,
for someone who wears it
exposed for everyone to see.
They taught me hugs can heal
most things.

I remember losing myself
in fathomless eyes, worrying for anyone
who tries to love the illustrious person
they are becoming.
Awkwardly navigating a body
they have yet to love,

but I remember when cells merged
miraculous, becoming you. My child,

I will always fight
to make sure your voice is heard,
to champion your every happiness.
Don't ever doubt, you
are the most perfect gift
exactly as you are.

Permanent Ink

I fall in love
with the power of words.
Every day is like a newfound
affection. I love
only in permanent ink.

Hummingbird's Union

He plops down
on a dining room chair.
Scoots to the edge.
Leans over, grabs
his twelve-string hummingbird.

Laying her neck, stretched out
as if to rest in his arms. Soft
inlay, alabaster pearls adorn
her mahogany dress.

Thumb thumps against wood.
First strum, strings strain,
fingers cast a spell.
He becomes song—

biting lip, arching back.
A delicious ditty drips
from his mouth.
Fingers fondle frets;
together, hypnotizing us
with his riff.

Jazzed ecstasy dances in his eyes
as hands pluck and drum.
She hums, bending to his desire
for her to come alive.

Chapter Five

WILDFLOWERS

AUREATE *(adj.) - Pertaining to the fancy or flowery words used by poets.*

Who Plucks from My Pages?

Maybe you hate
pants, can never find
your glasses,
and keep my book
on your nightstand, peeking
out from under
your own worn journal.
It lays ragged and bent,
pages dogeared or bookmarked
with a gum wrapper and pressed flowers.
You blacked out one page,
to make your own poem.

Perhaps my book sits
on your lover's
bookshelf, since your first
I love you. When you sat
together on the couch
and read poetry all day.
It rained nonstop;
the house lost power twice.
You saved the best
poems for candlelight
and fucked as thunder
began to crash.

It is conceivable you savor
malted whiskey from a tall,
bottom-heavy glass.
It feels big yet subtle
in how it dominates your

mouth. You tease yourself
with delay. Until you've had two
sips before opening
my book to the middle;
breathing in deep, searching
for what you cannot
put your finger on.
Hoping to catch
a feeling on a breath
and have your soul
quenched.

Likely, you are an explorer,
who asks the clerk
for forbidden things,
preferring to read rebels.
Oh, how you meander,
in hidden corners
of bookshops waiting
for your gut to stop you
among stacks. Trace fingers over
rows and rows, hoping for
a connection.
Whisper titles in a séance
inviting authors
to speak to you.
For connection
to a heart sparked
by kinship,
where no words hide.

Boundaries

She stands in the corner, pretending
to be a bookshelf—quiet, reserved.
Trying to protect herself;
war, all around.
She argues with herself
in frustration, not knowing
if she should wear armor as protection
or offer bare, loving arms to the world.
Her worth only in healing others.
Often draining her, leaving emptiness.
She longs for ears to hear,
arms to comfort.
She is always there
for others.
What about me? she thinks.
Replace the pain
she absorbs from the world.
Her boundaries feel
more like a box to lock herself in;
protecting her from enemies
she never wanted to fight.
No, a foreign word on her tongue.
She always complies.
Raped of all but her internal light, she sits
silent,
waiting to be rescued
from boundaries she has drawn in sand
that disappear in the wind.

The When

I remember when, that
exact instant.
Eyes met and
I smiled, instead
of shunning away.
Accepting this gaze,
lacking usual judgment,
scrutiny or agenda.
Just the hint
of a smile
in the corner of
a mouth.
Allowing worth, value,
and finally, acceptance.
In that moment
I knew.
Now every time
our eyes meet
I breathe whole.
In love with
who I have become—
this strong, beautiful
woman
in the mirror.

Mine

Alone.
Finally, alone.
Door closed and locked.
Lying in bed, my fingers slide
down, low
until they reach
their destination.

Skin there, warm and wet.
Oh, so very wet.
Slowly, I caress
the key that unlocks
what I dearly long for.
Fingers wander across
exposed flesh, taking
careful time.
Intensity builds;
heart racing, breath short.
I am immersed in pleasure
so intense
my body shudders.

I feel only pleasure
A second of breath-
easing sensitive
throbbing;
a beautiful pain behind.

Fingers move rapidly.
In and out; out and in.
They move in rhythmical balance,
a perfectly struck piano chord.

The pleasure tunes my body
into a world of melodic genius.
Slick walls increase speed
into manic euphoria.

My world turns into
unimaginable feats.
My head throws back,
and laughter escapes my mouth.
Sheets are saturated,
I am out of breath,
satisfied.
Then,
life resumes.

Woman

    soft gentle skin

    hidden secrets

    treasures unbound

    curves that capture

    imagination

    loving

    caring

    gives the gift

    of life

    and hope

    the future

    belongs to her

    in her

    because of her

    you dream

Writer's Block

I find myself trapped,
unable to explore
the words hidden
behind muddled thoughts.
I am a void of inspiration.
The bite of this loss
feels like nothingness.
I am numb.
Blocked.
The words cannot flow;
they disappear.
Knots fill my stomach.
I am flustered with this resistance.
Scared to cherish my own worth,
unworthy of this crown
placed on my head.
I watch, as it falls to the floor,
only to make no sound.
The deafening silence
is the peak of my frustration.
Where did all the words go?
I chisel at this impossible barrier blocking
all I am trying to convey.
A mountain of nothingness.
My blessings feel
like someone else's life.
Forced on like a dress
too small to breathe in.
I cling to the page
hoping the words appear.
But the knots grip
and twist and block.

Words

Should be taken and examined upon fingertips.
Drank until drunk upon the beauty of each syllable.
Should be whispered on bared souls.
Marry people to each other's minds.

Words should be looked at as cures.
Contemplated intensely to see
the beauty they form, the colors they paint
the heavens and the wind.
Should heal the broken heart, body, and mind.

Words should be held in reverence of their power.
Speak when not spoken.
Be expressed through a knowing glance,
and spoken with integrity *always*.

Words should titillate the recesses of your mind.
Fill the tongue with declarations so big
they pour out as a pledge of love.
Avoid gossip, tattling, and hearsay.
Cure tear-stained cheeks.

Words should be respected. Admired. Worshipped.
Held in devotion and astonishment.
Be taken slowly, seep into the brain and soul.
They should guarantee happiness
and right wrongs instead of poems.

The Library

A library is unparalleled
in its peculiarities,
its originality.
Its strange depths
and unexpected shallows.

Magic and science, evil eyes
and saints' lives
in a labyrinth of imagery
and icons and memory.

Inhale the damp, earthy aroma
of aging books.
Imagine specters
in the aisles haunting
their tomes. Dark

dusty shelves of forgotten
fables and bygone times,
occasionally examined
by someone seeking time
travel in solitude.

I come to study the oddity
of this place. History lives
here—ancient, old and local.

Searching for a secret
nook for privacy
among quiet pages.
Finding perfection in a small table,

two chairs, and dull lighting.
Exquisite in its loneliness.

Leaving my journal, I wander
through sections, browsing
for a familiar read
or something new
to spark inspiration.

Marveling through aisles, fingertips
grace over books, thick
with dreams. A treasure
catches my eye, hidden almost
on a lower shelf.
A book half the size of others.

Gold inlay almost gone
from age, it cracks
open and I know
no one has touched
these sheets in decades.

Delicate butterfly wing pages.
Petite words I trace, holding
it open with my thumb,
returning to the table
completely immersed.
Scribbling scrawls on the page of my journal,
and time waxes forgotten.

Moments

Ocean offers me a palette.
Every hue of lovely blue swirls of green
mixed with soft brown sand
topped off salted white foam.

People speak in hushed tones
to not let the joy of crashing waves
ruin this moment.
Sudden yelp of glee as we watch
a surfer's perfect wave.
Peaceful contentment on every face.
    Tides
shift
as worshippers take
first steps towards jubilation.
This church of souls' powerful connection.
Waves making rag dolls of people in the breaks.
They live for the moment right before
the anticipation
    of
        the
            fall.
Ocean taking away adult troubles
leaves only the quest for one more
and another.
Smiles, soul deep,
cannot be washed away.
Leave wet bliss
on the faces of graced rider.
Time s l o w s
in these m o m e n t s

as if to savor
every second
as a moment.
Every
      moment,
            an
                    eternity.
Lost in the dance
of whitecaps and spray.

No Name

My first thoughts of *It*—
no name, just a thing.
Curious hands learn body,
a mystery opening between legs.
It was never talked about,
held no value, was not special.
Was not meant to be
respected or ignored or just be.

Mom said, *Keep your hands away, dirty girl.*
Always self-conscious and wondering,
do I reject this part of me? *It*,
naughty, and I had no idea why.
What was wrong with *It*?
Society says, *only let a man who says*
he loves you touch It…after marriage.

A high school boy defiled *It*
with his fist, with a beer bottle.
I remember
blood;
not screaming.
Teens gossiping about *It*, after,
in halls, whispering *slut*–'cuz boys brag—
He said, *I wanted it.*
so obviously, I am.

I made excuses for everything
about *It*,
to men who could
not care less.

Who tried to control *It/me*,
by using *It/me* for their pleasure.

Never talking to other women.
Assuming they are living in skin
more comfortable than mine.
It, a shameful, disgusting thing.
No positive role models
or memory related to *It*.

I survived.
Learned forced touches
are not love.
Had a funeral for impure skeletons,
built an altar of sensual adoration.
Filled it with self-esteem.
Fed myself patience, confidence, and custody.
Realized the well-being of body and mind.
Invested in my own worth,
making self-love exquisite.

Addicted to the power now
of valuing myself.

My identity no longer tied
to the satisfaction of anyone
else—claiming a name for *It*.

Hello, my name is Heather!

Lessons from Life

Remember it is always darkest before the dawn
　　　　　　　　　　　　－ Florence + The Machine

I have learned sometimes
I was my own abuser,
careening out of control
on a path of sabotage. Forgiveness
is meant for myself first.
Healing has no concept of time.

I have learned that not every fight
needs a battle; I was not made
for war. Death is not something
to wait for. Life is about connection,
education, is a journey of continual
growth.

I have learned to stop looking back
at paths not taken.
To not drop my burdens, and lade
myself with others'.

I have learned that it is okay to ask for help.
Let me say that again
It. Is. Okay. To. Ask. For. Help.
It is not okay to pretend. I am only fooling
myself.

I have learned that being heard
doesn't mean I have to be loud,
but I will be loud for what I believe in!

Silence, like cancer, kills!

I have learned I am
comfortable with who I am,
most days. Not defined by anyone.
Labels are for clothing.

I have learned that being funny doesn't
mean I have
to be the joke.
Only children have no
concept of regret.
Hugs have power; crying has it too.
The love I require is right in the mirror.

I have learned expression
is survival; I
bleed on paper to breathe.
Darkness is temporary, I now carry pen
as a flashlight.

I have learned that I am an atheist.
It's okay if you're not.
I am a feminist. It is not okay
if you are not.
Integrity is everything.

I have learned
growth requires raw - real – truth.
I am a Survivor, which
means I am strong.
I am fiercely loved. I trust in
that love completely.
My family is my universe,
my sun, moon, and stars.

I have learned words/ have
the power/ you give them.
To listen more than to speak.
To savor a moment, turn it into
a memory. Laughter should
never be held back.
I was born.

I have learned I am worthy
of this life.
I am worthy
of love.
I am worthy.

Writer

I write to breathe; it's the only way I exhale.
I write for the little girl silenced,
questions left unanswered.

I write to live.
Lungs exposed, heaving chest.
Bleeding ink. Turning
inside and out.

I write for a lifeline—
a shared moment.
To feel alive,
know I am not alone.

I write as a sword against monsters.
An exorcism of demons
to turn nightmares into dreams.
Control my version of my own story.

Writing freezes time and extends it.
Is my champion, caregiver, and deity.

I write for blind eyes and deaf ears.
To release burdens with the flip of a page.
Rephrase the world in a way I can grasp.

I speak what I write
because someone told me to shut up
and I never do what I'm told.

I write away stereotypes.
Take away shackles.

My voice belongs to me!

I am never afraid of what I write.
I am terrified of what I don't write.
I hid in notebooks, gathering dust for too long.
I write because this is not a choice for me.

It
is
me.

PETALS OF GRATITUDE

RASTROPHILIOPUSTROCITY (*n.*) - *A spontaneous combustion of creative spark, that is followed by action in order to manifest and bring into existence.*

Acknowledgements:

Thank you to the following publications, books and journals, in which some of these poems first appeared or are appearing in slightly different forms:

Prachya Review, "Monster Squatter" & "I Took a Shower Today"
Inquietudes Literary Journal, "Words"
Poetry Breakfast, "Talk to Me"
Anti-Heroin Chic. "A Room too Small" and "Rocks"
For Women Who Roar #MeToo e-book, "#Believed"
San Diego Poetry Annual, "How to Give a Flower"
A Teenager's Guide to Feminism, Pear Shaped Press, "Lessons from Life"

Thank you!

To the poets and friends who advocated by offering advice, proofreading, suggestions, edits, rewrites, tissues, and hugs; I can't thank each of you enough for being so kind and gentle with my heart. For feeding my spirit and inspiring my soul. I am forever grateful for who you are and the gift of your help in creating this amazing book. It's everything I wanted it to be and more because of your efforts.

To the wonderful souls who told me to love myself, write about what scares me, and be true in what I say…I did, I do, I always will. Thank you for helping me see myself whole.

Notes:

The word LOVE appears 47 times in this book, which is perfect. I've never felt good enough or deserving of the word. It took me into my 40s to truly love myself and realize that when others say, "I love you," they mean it.

Fine Art, written in 2012, was inspired by a work by Kevin Flint. You can find his work here: www.kevinflint.com

Meditation is about Carbon Canyon Regional Park in Yorba Linda, California.

Catfish & Hushpuppies is about Greers Ferry Dam in Heber Springs, Arkansas.

About the Author

This is 4-year-old me.
Mousy and I
are still tight. I just want
to say to that
little girl
"Look, sweetheart, you're a poet!"

Get in Touch!

Instagram @ohpoetic1
Facebook @heatherpeasepoetry
www.heatherpease.com

www.ingramcontent.com/pod-product-compliance
Lightning Source LLC
Chambersburg PA
CBHW050914160426
43194CB00011B/2405